Dime Store
Decorating
using flea market
finds with style

Dime Store
Decorating
using flea market
finds with style

Jill Williams Grover

Sterling Publishing Co., Inc. New York
A Sterling/Chapelle Book

Chapelle Ltd.

Owner: Jo Packham

Editor: Linda Orton

Staff: Areta Bingham, Kass Burchett, Marilyn Goff,
Holly Hollingsworth, Susan Jorgensen, Barbara Milburn,
Karmen Quinney, Leslie Ridenour, Cindy Stoeckl,
Gina Swapp, Sara Toliver, Kristi Torsak

Photography: Kevin Dilley, for Hazen Imaging, Inc.
                 Scot Zimmerman for Scot Zimmerman Photography

Library of Congress Cataloging-in-Publication

Grover, Jill Williams.
    Dime store decorating : using flea market finds with style / Jill Grover.
        p. cm.
    Includes index.
    ISBN 0-8069-7493-1
        1. House furnishings. 2. Interior decoration. 3. Flea markets. I. Title.

    TX311 .G75 2001
    747--dc21

                                                        00-053789

10 9 8 7 6 5 4 3 2 1

A Sterling/Chapelle Book

Published by Sterling Publishing Company, Inc.
387 Park Avenue South, New York, NY 10016
© 2001 by Chapelle Ltd.
Distributed in Canada by Sterling Publishing
% Canadian Manda Group, One Atlantic Avenue, Suite 105
Toronto, Ontario, Canada M6K 3E7
Distributed in Great Britain and Europe by Cassell PLC
Wellington House, 125 Strand, London WC2R 0BB, England
Distributed in Australia by Capricorn Link (Australia) Pty Ltd.
P.O. Box 704, Windsor, NSW 2756 Australia
Printed in China
All Rights Reserved

Sterling ISBN 0-8069-7493-1

Every effort has been made to ensure that all of the information in this book is accurate.

If you have any questions or comments, please contact:

Chapelle Ltd., Inc.
P.O. Box 9252
Ogden, UT 84409

Phone: (801) 621-2777
FAX: (801) 621-2788
e-mail: chapelle@chapelleltd.com
website: www.chapelleltd.com

flea-market pin

discount-store scarf

dime-store jewelry

dime-store bow ties

discount-store earrings
for cuff links

thrift-store belt

Dime-store accessorizing is exciting and enchanting!

Jill Grover, an interior designer, is the mother of three and resides with her husband and children in Northern Utah. She has appeared locally—as well as nationally—on various television programs, sharing advice on crafting and decorating.

She has made use of her creative talents as the author of *Scary Scenes for Halloween* and *Handmade Giftwrap, Bows, Cards and Tags.*

This book is dedicated to my husband Richard,
Thank you for making all my dreams come true!
I love you . . .

table of

contents

In *Dime Store Decorating,* I have presented new and unusual ideas for decorating with ordinary discounted items which can almost always be found in flea markets, dime stores, dollar stores, and thrift shops. Placing these found inexpensive "things" with your own personal treasures and collections adds new charm, stretches your budget, and gives you a creative touch when decorating your home.

Why not decorate with these low-cost items. They give you the opportunity to try something new or take a "decorating risk" without costing more than you can really afford. With this book, you will discover new ways to turn ordinary items into accents and accessories that are neither expected or predictable. It allows you the luxury to redecorate as often as you want by simply changing a few items which cost very little.

"Making something unexpected happen" is the concept behind *Dime Store Decorating,* much like when Maria in the *Sound of Music* made play clothes from bedroom curtains because children need play clothes not straitjackets. Decorating your home can echo just this philosophy of reflecting you, your life-style, and your good taste.

It is a joy to decorate in a delightful comfortable manner, to create a warm haven that speaks of the family as a whole and the family members as individuals. It is the wish of us all to create a place where happy hearts always come home and memories are made.

The way in which each dime-store or flea-market purchase is displayed, how it is used, and what you combine it with has everything to do with the success you will have in decorating your home with these inexpensive items. Hints for guaranteed success are: 1. Look for a common denominator in the accessories you already have to display with these new items. 2. Buy, so new and old items can be placed in groupings by color, shape, subject, or theme. 3. Buy whatever catches your attention when you see it, because it is a one-of-a-kind or a closeout item and it may not be there when you return. 4. Use your imagination and do not be timid or insecure. If it doesn't work, you can give it away or put it away for another day and another idea.

right with
white

Glass Light-shade Art

Who said light shades have to cover light bulbs and earrings have to be worn?

When I purchased these light shades at a local thrift store, the largest shade had been painted red on the inside of the glass. I used paint thinner and a rag to remove the paint, with the end result being a light pink cast to the glass. Covering the hole in the center and hanging the shades was my next challenge. I had purchased some ornate earrings at the same thrift store, so I decided they would look fabulous while covering the center hole. A length of wire was bent in half and threaded through the two holes in a large white button. The wire ends were passed through the center hole of the shade and through the earring, then pulled tight, fitting the button and earring snugly against the light shade. The wire ends were twisted together against the button to secure the button and earring. The remaining wire ends were then used to hang the light shades on the wall.

15

Baluster Mirror

Unusable discarded tables and chairs with turned legs, or old banister balusters are an easy find at flea markets and thrift stores. By cutting them in half, gluing them onto a plain flat frame; painting them with burnt umber acrylic paint; applying a crackle medium, according to manufacturer's instructions, and then coating the entire surface with an antique white acrylic paint, you have created a vintage mirror with architectural elements and design.

Baluster Candlesticks

Another designer idea for old chair legs or balusters is antique candlesticks. The wide end must be flat, sanded smooth, and a hole large enough to hold a candle cup drilled in the top of each baluster. Once the candle cup is glued into place, the candlesticks are ready for honey-colored hand-dipped candles.

16

Crystal Candleholders

Dainty cut-crystal glasses are difficult to use in today's family. What is a teenager or the man-of-the-house to do with such a thing? They are also just too pretty to store inside the cupboard. So why not use them to add that shimmering touch to a small coffee table? Simply take your prettiest goblets and place a candle in each, or a tiny bit of water and a rose in the odd one. To create a designer display, stack two glass bottoms together and combine with other crystal and glass treasures that you want to use and enjoy.

Bright White Chandelier

The chandelier in my dining room is adorned with metal leaves that are painted bright white. This is a perfect piece for me because on occasions when I need to feel uncomplicated, I leave the chandelier as is. However, on those special days or evenings when something new must be added, I decorate to my hearts content. One evening when my husband and I were having a romantic dinner for just the two of us, I wound bouncing icicles—that I had found months before at a Christmas closeout sale—around the arms that hold the candle lights. With the lights turned down and the glow from the candles on the table, the reflections in the icicles were magic.

Hanging Lights

These white metal lights have been hanging over the island in my kitchen since we built our house. I still like them as much today as I did the day I selected them. However, every once in a while I need a little change, so I glued crystal mosaic pieces at random around the shades with jewelry glue.

Every time I walk up or down our stairs I smile because it is then that I see the wall that displays our favorite family photographs. It is here that the stories of love and wonderful memories are told and retold time and time again.

When we finished our new home, I knew this would be the perfect place for our family photo wall. It was important to me that each one of the pictures be taken by myself or my children—a professional must never be used. It is the memory and the feeling of the moment that counts, not the technical know-how of a professional. To make this number of frames and mats affordable, I measured the wall to see how many I would ultimately need, I waited for a "big" sale, and purchased enough frames at the same time to completely cover the wall. When I saw a favorite photograph during the many months in which these photos were taken, I would have it enlarged at my photo supply store. After it was placed behind the mat, the person who took the photograph would write a short meaningful caption on the mat with a permanent black pen.

Whenever I stop to look, the memories come flooding back. I especially adore the one my son took of my father. He passed on a few months later, making this one of the most priceless photos on our wall. My other favorite is "End of a perfect day." It was taken at the end of one of those "red letter" days on a family vacation to Oregon that was loved by us all.

Stacked Photo Frames

On the end table in my living room, I have placed seashells that were collected at the beach, an old vase found at a Saturday morning garage sale and filled with silk flowers and spanish moss, and more of my favorite family photographs. I had three hinged frames that I bought at a buy-two-get-one-free sale. I stacked one on top of another and fastened them together with brackets for additional stability. By stacking the frames, I have created a piece that is not only important to me, but that makes a statement in my small array of treasures. The keepsakes on this table are inexpensive, sentimental, and easily changed with the coming of cold fall days when acorns will replace the shells and branches full of autumn leaves will fill my vase.

Petite Picture Frames

Sometimes one just is not enough—translation: repetition is one of many keys that unlocks the secrets to designer decorating.

The flowers were removed from a series of girls' miniature barrettes and hot-glued to tiny plastic picture frames. Favorite family photos were cropped or reduced and placed inside of each frame.

Small Vases

Big is not always better—translation: miniatures draw the eye in their direction making them a focal point, because of their scale.

Small decorative bottles were filled with water, a pinch of glitter was added for sparkle, and fresh miniature roses were placed inside to complete my tiny, but very cute hall-table display.

Telephone Stand

A plain white set of drawers is just a plain white set of drawers unless something unexpected is added.

I needed this chest of drawers to fill an empty space in my hallway. However, when it was placed there, it looked very plain, very ordinary, and very predictable—and no one liked it very much. A friend came to my home and suggested that I give it some color—but I didn't want to paint it and I couldn't quite decide what to do. Consequently, it sat in the hall for a week or two while we all looked at it, thought about it, and contemplated what to do with it. Then on a Monday afternoon while I was visiting a friend, she asked if I had a place for these extra, unmatched, oversized knobs she had purchased and no longer liked. They were perfect for my set of plain white drawers! They were over-sized, which is somewhat of a traditional design contradiction, they were colorful but temporary and could easily be changed, they were exactly what we were all trying to find!

Plate Rack

To add a little height and additional interest to my newly created piece of "art furniture" in my hallway, I hung a plate rack and filled it with pieces that are important to me. Some of which is important to me is my family, our farm, and the wheat that is grown on our farm. I had a favorite picture of my son Levi in one of our fields of wheat, eating a popsicle. I framed it in a plain white frame and glued colored flat marbles on all sides. The plate is one I love and that I simply had to have. On the top of my telephone stand, I placed books I had found during my many flea-market Saturdays—all of which have wheat or something related to our farming or family in the title. And of course, because I love stars, one of my many star boxes sits on top.

When winter comes I will change the photo to one of the other children outside playing in the snow, the plate will be one that Levi made for me for Christmas when he was in the third grade, and the books will be of our favorite Christmas stories and carols.

Any room with a fireplace is the ultimate retreat. It is a haven for private reflection, a place to create secret dreams, an enclave where evenings can be spent with family and friends. It is here you can wrap yourself in the quiet of the moment or the laughter that fills the room.

During the summer months when a fire is not needed for warmth—but the firelight is wanted for a soft warm glow while the breeze blows through the open windows—why not place pillar candles on the hearth. To stack them, use unusual blocks of some sort. These are dice from an old lawn game, and to add just the right touch of sparkle, drape faceted-surface glass jewelry around some of the candles to twinkle in the candlelight. Now, winter or summer, you can enjoy a favorite time and place.

It is here around the fireplace that you surround yourself with those you love, the treasures you have collected, and the light of the fire. It is here, in this unusually small area, that you can create a style that is truly your own. It can be a fireplace mantel that is the essence of simple homespun luxury, a work of art that is the epitome of sophisticated ease, or one which walks the line between silly and chic.

Tissue Box Covers

A favorite photo of our family hangs above our fireplace mantel—it is the center of my decorating in our family room. To celebrate the coming of the summer months, I pulled an unexpected tiny detail from the picture and used it as the theme to decorate the mantel—the black bow tie.

I took four black-and-white polka-dotted tissue box covers, turned them upside down, and lined them up across the mantel. I added pots of perky flowers, and tied a bow tie around one.

Wastebasket Candles

On the end of each of my "vases," I used unconventional candle-holders. These are clear bathroom wastebaskets which are filled three-quarters full with rock salt to secure the tapers that are lit on quiet, almost romantic evenings at home.

The collecting of "things" is essential for any lover of bargains and flea-market finds. The pieces may be "like items" found in a dollar store, whose price was irresistible. They may be collected over a series of visits to several different garage sales, or they may be given as gifts from family and friends who know you love such "things." And contrary to the old adage "too much of a good thing . . . ," you can never have too much when it comes to the collections of that which fascinates you.

Collections can be different items that are alike because of color (pieces of Blue Willow Ware), items that are made from the same material but different in shape (crystal candlesticks), or items that relate to a theme (cowboy anything). I have collections that fall into each of these categories, and I add to them whenever I can. Once I had decided to collect white vintage vases, I began exploring local thrift shops and second-hand stores. Much to my surprise, all but one of these vases was found at the same shop. Each Monday morning, I fill a different vase with fresh flowers to begin our week anew.

Everything white is always right, because white symbolizes that which is clean, crisp, pure, and serene in the world. A collection of items that are white in the guest bath of our home offers our family, friends, and overnight guests a few simple embellishments and stylings that create a wonderful mood. These items are there, ready for each in the stolen moments when they wish to pamper both their body and their soul.

Jars filled with scented soaps, beautiful bottles filled with sweet-smelling lotions and indulgent creams, towels wrapped with ribbons to resemble expensive gifts, and stars shining with little white lights set the mood. These are what are placed on the pristine, aged white shelves in our bath to help those who wish to partake in a mini celebration of ancient bathing rituals and self-indulgence.

The jars on the top shelf are filled with homemade bath salts. There are recipes that are complicated and long with items that are difficult to find, or you can use a simple one of equal parts Epsom salt and sea salt. A few drops of your favorite essential oil or perfume will add a subtle, soothing scent, and soap shavings can be added on top—for no reason at all. For the sheer fun of it, make a bouquet of toothbrushes in a glass, hang your favorite shower curtain clip on a jar, and place those often-needed cotton swabs in an old-fashioned apothecary jar.

Stenciled Stars

What better accent color can there be than brilliant gold for a soft serene white-on-white bathroom? Varied sizes of metallic gold stars were stenciled as a border along the top of a plain white wall, giving this bathroom an almost heavenly touch.

Bath Bottles

Decorative bottles, purchased at a dollar store, were emptied and refilled with gold bath soap, scented to smell like spring rain.

Photo Soap Dish

A ceramic star picture frame, purchased long ago, now doubles as a soap dish. It contains a laminated photograph that is covered with glass on the front, and a piece of cardboard wrapped in part of an old shower curtain on the back. In this way, it can be used by dirty hands on a daily basis and will have to be replaced only occasionally.

stars

and jars

"Twinkle, twinkle little star; how I wonder what you are"—it is the mystery and the magic of the star that so appeals to anyone of any age.

I made this large star wreath to light the way and welcome family, friends, and guests to our home. Five dowels were placed in a star position and the ends were wired together. A few grapevines, cut from the backyard, were wired to the base, followed by white twinkle lights. More grapevines were wired in place to fill in the empty spaces, and to cover the electrical cords.

We hang this, regardless of the season, because the message and the magic is always the same.

s t a r s

Rusty Star Candleholders

On a Tuesday morning, while shopping with a friend at a famous closeout store, I fell in love with these rusty tin star-shaped candleholders. Buying one didn't seem like quite enough—after all, at the price they were marked, it was almost like giving them away—and I could always use them as gifts for our neighbors. However, as does sometimes happen, when I got them home, I couldn't bear to part with even one of them. To justify buying so many, I decided to use them to decorate the family room. To the back of each piece, I attached a picture-hanging hook, then hung them on nails above my shutters. The hardest part was measuring to make certain they were even from top to bottom and side to side.

42

Christmas without trees and stars and all that glitters in their light would be unthinkable. For this season of hope and love and peace, the trees in the forest, the stars that crown them or those that are in the heavens, and the jewels that are the gifts of kings are the essence of the traditions and the stories of Christmas.

I love all of these—so each Christmas, I add trees and stars and jewels and gifts to our holiday celebration.

The ornaments were made the old-fashioned way from beads and jewels and gold cutouts, pinned with straight pins onto satin thread balls—the same as those hung on Christmas trees 30 years ago. They remind me of the homes of my mother's friends when I was much younger than I am now. I am certain I had just as much fun making them as they did, so very long ago.

holidays

Golden Christmas Trees

These golden trees were purchased at the end-of-the-season sale last year. This year they were wrapped with vintage jewelry—some of which I bought here and there, and some of which was given to me by family and friends.

Gold Gift Box

This inexpensive plain box was purchased for a special gift, so it needed a special touch. The first thing I did was to paint the box with metallic gold paint. The lid was then sprayed with an adhesive and glitter was sprinkled over the adhesive. The star was originally purchased to crown one of our trees, but it looked just right on top of the box, so until the gift was given on Christmas eve, the star stayed where you see it.

Both cooks and collectors love jars, bottles, baskets, boxes, containers, or whatever can actually hold items used in cooking on their shelves. They also love spending time in the kitchen, which is the heart of the home and a perfect place to remind everyone who enters there what being a family is all about.

Sometimes you find the most unique items, and they are so inexpensive, that you buy them because you are certain you will find a use for them. That was the case with these paint roller inserts. I hung them between my countertop and cupboards to hold my favorite recipes and photographs.

countertops

Canisters

Closeout and dollar stores' stock changes rapidly, so one needs to frequent these stores on a regular basis to seek out any new merchandise. I shop all of my favorite stores often, and when I see something I like, I buy it—which was the case with these canisters and star cookie cutters. For a while they were in my cupboard, but now I use them on the counter to hold supplies and brighten my day.

Picture Frame Mosaic

One just such way to show your family how much you care is to save all of the broken dishes and make a mosaic out of them. I made this one from some of my favorite cups and saucers, and each time I look at it, it brings back all of the memories that are associated with the family dinners where these dishes were used—it matters not that the dishes are no longer in one piece.

Pastel Water Vases

Counters, shelves, tabletops, consoles—all are places to put the things you love. I am always putting the flowers from my garden in unusual vases on any surface where there is room. This collection of various sized vases and glassware is filled with pastel-colored water that not only matches the subtle color of the roses, but is scented the same as well. The color is a few drops of food coloring and the scent is from oils found at the craft store.

Sundae Dishes

I love anything that is painted pastel—flowers, glasses, ice cream—and here are all three. Because these shaded sundae glasses represent all that is summer to me, I placed them on my counter to be filled with flowers and candy. I even surrounded them with tiny, jeweled silver frames. When the sun shines in my window early in the morning, the light through the glasses throws prisms on my tile, and my day is filled with the soft colors of the rainbow.

Shell Flowerpots

When I saw these shell flowerpots, I knew I had to have them—all of them. One or two would never do because they could be used in so many ways, for so many reasons. On top of my picnic table for a summer "beach" party, I filled the pots with sand and rested a candle in each. I also took a series of the shells we had gathered at the beach, drilled holes in some, and strung them on ribbon for the end of the table, then the remainder were rested against the candles.

Pails of Light

In my garden, I have hidden several small tables on which to put things among my flowers. For many of our summer parties, I have filled galvanized garden buckets—which I paint with my favorite colors of latex paint—with water, a variety of fresh flowers, and an assortment of floating candles. When placed on the hidden tables, they are raised just enough to be easily seen by but out of the way of my guests. The theme is as easy to change as the water.

jars

What all collectors of junk-store treasures and flea-market finds have in common is a lot of stuff. When I brought all of these jars, bottles, and glass chimneys home, my family was convinced that I now had too much stuff. But when I filled the jars and bottles with the sand and seashells from our latest trip to the beach, carefully placed candles of all sizes—one in each jar—and covered the opening with a glass chimney or a glass light fixture, all my family could say was, "you've done it again, mom!" The glass chimneys were once used as light shades on old chandeliers, and the glass fixtures are the coverings from old hanging or ceiling lights. I love this collection because it is a concept that is all mine I have never seen it—before—anywhere.

The top of my mantel is one of my favorite places to display those collections that are breakable or are among my very favorites. When I purchased these mosaic vases and candleholders, I knew they would be perfect above the light of the fire in my music room.

In each mosaic vase, I placed a string of white Christmas lights and a bouquet of glass rods that I found at the stained-glass supply store. The mosaic candleholders each hold a small votive candle. Interspersed with my new glass pieces are a variety of clear goblets, vases, and glassware. I again filled these with colored water and dripless tapers. When the lights are dimmed, the candles are lit, and the music is playing, this is a wonderful place to be.

One other trait that all collectors have in common is that they never do stop collecting. Once you fall in love with a style, a color, or a theme, the philosophy that "too much is never enough" is that by which you live.

The nice part of collecting is that you can display the beginnings of your collection, a portion of your collection, or the entire collection—it matters not. An example of this is the two photographs to the left. In the first photograph the blue objects that the collector has displayed are on her family-room coffee table. As each new piece is added to the collection, it is added to the top of the coffee table as well. When there become too many, some can be taken away and stored for a while, some can be added to other collections, and some can be left where they are.

Cake Vase

I placed a blue-and-white patterned plate on top of a vase for an unusual and vintage-style cake plate. If a permanent adhesion is desired, use china glue; if not, simply lift the plate from the vase when cutting and serving.

quite bright

I have always wanted to visit Holland to see the colors of the tulips as they grow in the fields, and to bring back a trunk filled with painted wooden shoes. When I found these clogs in the thrift store, I made certain they came home with me. They bring to our front porch the colors of the fields of Holland and a welcome invitation—as well as a subtle reminder for guests—to please come in, but please wipe your feet before you do. For a special family gathering, I even placed tiny pots of fresh flowers and votive candles in each of the shoes, to help light the way to our front door.

Fashion has always exerted a major influence on home decor; and just as there are an infinite number of choices for the perfect prom dress, there are as many ways to dress your dining room.

When choosing a fashion style for this month's dining room ensemble, do so with a touch of color and an eclectic charm that might be somewhat new for you. In place of a traditional tablecloth, try taking two box-pleated cafe curtains and attaching them as the "ruffle" on the edge of the table. When I was redoing my dining room for Mother's Day, I had purchased two identical dresses at a vintage thrift store. I hung one on the wall and used the other to make pillows for the chairs. With such ornate additions, the chairs looked too heavy, so "chair trains" were created from sheer cur-

tains. I then draped inexpensive beaded necklaces around the chandelier to accent the colors on the table. Some of the strings were jewelry from discount stores, and some I made myself, by stringing beads onto long pieces of fish line. They are difficult to see, but I even placed beaded ponytail holders under each sconce on my chandelier, for a little added sheer delight.

Daily Planner

Most families today seem to have too much to do and too little time. To help organize our days, I created an over-sized calendar in our kitchen. A common piece of sheet metal was painted with chalkboard paint and nailed to the wall. A frame was created with strips of molding which was nailed over the edges of the metal.

60

Each family member has their own color of chalk, so that they know instantly which activities and appointments during the day apply to them.

The clocks were purchased at a going-out-of-business sale. To make a point of being punctual, I hung one for each of us above the chalkboard. When the children move away, the clocks can each be set for different time zones.

Magnets

Because our family calendar is made of metal, important papers, invitations, and schedules can be held in place by magnets. As a family activity one Monday night, each member of the family made their own magnet. Each of us was required to bring our own favorite "things" that could have small round magnets glued to the back. Laci brought metal lady bugs that she had on the top of her dresser. I, of course, had my collection of vintage jewelry. It would be easy to use other items such as napkin rings, cards, marbles, or plastic toys. I supplied each with powerful, small round magnets that I found at the craft store to be hot-glued to the back of their treasures.

Terra-cotta Charger

A large ordinary terra-cotta saucer was used as a charger on my Mother's Day table. These accented the glass plates that I decoupaged with pin-dot fabric and used as a second charger. Decoupaged plates are easy to do with reverse glass decoupage glue, which can be found at all craft supply stores. Simply follow the manufacturer's instructions.

Homemade Muffins

For our Mother's Day brunch, I made oversized muffins in small cake pans and served them in bright white coffeepot liners. On top of each, I placed a dollop of whipping cream, flavored with a hint of almond and topped with a cherry. Fresh fruit and lemonade—served in cute frog glasses that are actually bathroom tumblers, with matching straws cut to different lengths—finished off my plate.

Ceramic Purse Place Cards

If you look closely on the opposite page, you can see the tiny porcelain purses on the plates. These were found in a funky old-fashioned dime store years ago, and saved for just such an occasion. I made them into place cards by attaching strung alphabet beads to spell out each guest's name. Each was then given to my guests as a small thank-you gift for sharing my day.

Mugs With Garden Gloves

Because it is my Mother's Day table—and because my personal passion is gardening—I tucked pairs of my favorite gardening gloves into each cup for my guests. To hold the gloves and napkins in the cup, I wrapped black-and-white polka-dotted ribbon around plastic bracelets for napkin rings, and placed them in the cup. The napkins were made from a larger tablecloth, which made them much less expensive than purchasing single cotton napkins.

63

Wastebasket Vase

I love green frogs, and when I purchased the bathroom mugs with frogs on them, I also brought home the wastebasket. Because it is just too cute to hold trash, I used it in the center of my table to hold fresh flowers from the garden. I filled the wastebasket with ice so the stems would be hidden and the frog would be more noticeable.

Pedestal Serving Dish

Two plates and a cola mug were secured with hot glue to make this colorful serving platter. I placed an inexpensive ponytail holder around the mug base to add a splash of color, and glass frogs that had been placed in the freezer, helped keep the limes fresh and cold.

Polka-dotted Servers

The large wooden fork and spoon were dipped in paint and when dry, polka dots were applied by dipping a pencil eraser in contrasting paint and dotting the handles. I then tied each with a ribbon, so they were as pretty as they could be.

Strawberry Server

By hot-gluing an overturned mug to a plate, and a bowl atop the mug, another quaint and creative serving platter was made for a delightful and attractive addition to my table. By using hot glue, the platter can be made for temporary, but stable use. The hot glue can be pulled off easily when the meal is cleared from the table. For a more permanent use, china glue can be applied in lieu of hot glue.

Tumbler Candleholders

Black-and-white polka-dotted bathroom tumblers were turned upside down to make candleholders. Matching green votive candles were placed in the cupped bottom of the tumbler, and beaded ponytail holders were wrapped around the neck. After Mother's Day, I am going to place these in the window behind my sink to add a little color to an ordinary day.

Chair "Trains"

I found apple green curtains at a home decorating outlet and purchased them because I loved the color. Each curtain was cut in half and hemmed to make an elegant "train" for the backs of my dining room chairs. The loops used to tie the curtains on the rod were simply tied into bows, and T-pins were used to attach the "trains" to the chair backs.

Cheery Dish Towel Pillows

Cheery pillows were made for the dining room by stitching these charming dish towels together. The smaller of the two pillows is one dish towel folded in half and sewn together with three seams. The larger pillow is two dish towels sewn together. Before the seams were sewn, lace was glued to the underside of each edge. It is an inexpensive ten-minute project that can add color and pattern to any table setting.

Beaded fabric anything, has always been a favorite of mine; and because of its current popularity, it is now being used by designers everywhere for everything and it has become very expensive. One day while shopping at my favorite thrift store, I found two brand new dresses—price tags still attached—that had wonderful sequin bead-work over the entire jewel-toned dress. I immediately bought both, and hung one on the wall in my kitchen, because it seemed like an unexpected thing to do and the color and drape of the fabric was so beauti-ful. I cut the other dress up to make pillows for my dining room chairs and a table run-ner for the coffee table in my music room. I now have an art piece, four pillows, and a table runner, all for less than half of what I would have paid for one small designer pil-low with beadwork.

For reasons that I cannot explain, many women love to collect bottles. Sometimes each is filled with flowers from their garden, some are filled with perfumes and fancy oils, some hold a variety of items used in the kitchen for cooking, or sometimes they are just left empty.

I, like so many others, love bottles. Bottles of every color and kind. I have a collection of jewel-toned bottles in various shapes and sizes, which are filled with roses and dandelions that my son picks for me each Saturday morning; or they are topped off with unexpected household objects in place of the usual cork stoppers. An oversized marble, a curtain rod finial, a child's plastic bouncy ball, a feather, a rock-candy sucker, and an earring are just some of the items that I use.

Just as unexpected as the toppers or dandelions is the table runner that was made from the dress I found in a thrift store and the leopard-print lunch pail that, when set among the bottles, adds an unpredictable accent to one of my favorite collections. It isn't a bottle, but the large green glass vase is actually the shade from an old 50s' lamp I found, and the marble vases in blue and yellow always remind me of a summer day. This collection was made by gluing transparent marbles onto the outside of plain glass containers, using glass and bead glue. My favorite among these is the miniature bottle with a simple ring of marbles around the neck and filled with dandelions. My son made it especially for me to keep the fresh dandelions that he picks—which is reason enough to cherish it.

I can think of nothing that will bring a setting alive more immediately than flowers, nor anything that offers us a more spontaneous means of arranging the different areas we live in with greater interest, imagination, and sensitivity. And for the diversity of flowers in a home, one must have a variety of containers which will also offer endless possibilities for changing the areas in which we spend the days of our lives.

Containers are accent pieces that affect the color and the texture of the blossoms, as well as that indefinable state of mind—the mood. Flowers in glass containers take on the clarity of the glass, and those carefully placed in toothbrush tumblers—which are easy containers to find at bargain prices—are as fresh and disarming as a child's smile. Such holders make great vases because the toothbrush slots hold the flower stems in place perfectly, without having to wire them. When dime-store decorating, always use something for what it isn't and never hesitate to be a little unconventional—family and friends will love what you do!

Flower Candleholders

Line your window with perpetually blossoming flowers. These painted wineglasses and flowerpots—lined up along the window sill like so many potted flowers—are darling candleholders. Petals and blossoms were painted onto the outside of these wineglasses with acrylic paint, and small terra-cotta pots were painted in corresponding colors and sealed with a satin varnish. The glasses were then hot-glued to the inside rim of the pot, and the colors of the votives were picked to match the painted flowers.

Picture-hanging Drawer Pulls

Green acrylic drawer pulls were converted in an unconventional manner to wall hooks. They were then used to hang pictures made from sentimental greeting cards, received on special occasions from someone important. Beaded hair wraps were attached to the back of each frame and used to hang the pictures from the pulls.

Hear the music that chirps thru the air… And look at the stars, like you do… And know in your heart, my little girl, That I'm there and I've lit them for you.

Memories are made from places we've been, people we've known, and moments we've shared. Some memories bring a tear to your eye, a smile to your face, or a song to your heart. Some are meant to be told and retold, and some are meant to be kept quietly tucked away in your heart.

Many of the memories I hold most dear are retold here in this small corner, in an area between our kitchen and our family room. These vintage soda-shop seats were brought in and surrounded by treasures that I love. The two old window frames were collected from our farm and painted green. Artwork drawn by my son, a favored poster that was a gift from my husband, and meaningful illustrations from magazines, books, and greeting cards were taped behind the glass. A poem about stars, written by a friend in memory of my father, is stenciled around the window frames.

I have a special place in my heart for stars and use them whenever and wherever I can; because as a young child I thought the sound made by crickets came from the stars. My dad would come into the house in the evenings and say, "Jilly Pill, the stars are singing tonight." Then he would take me by the hand and we would go outside and, standing side-by-side, we would listen to the symphony of stars.

A child should have a room that makes him feel happy, comfortable, content, and safe—a personal retreat that belongs no one else. When decorating for children, I insist that their own personal space reflect what they do, who they are, and what they love. River, my youngest son, is one of those truly happy children that loves bright colors and fun things, so when decorating, we made certain that his room echoes all that he is.

River wanted a "Happy Jungle" bedroom, so leopard spots on the wall and jungle animals were the place to begin. Bright jungle colors of green, red, blue, and yellow were brought into play wherever we could. The leopard spots were stenciled onto the wall, using three colors of acrylic paint, and the animals were brought together and arranged "just so" on his bed.

Covered Storage Boxes

An inexpensive yet decorative storage space is easily made by covering cardboard boxes with paper or fabric selected by your child. Make certain to wrap the lid separately and to tie the package with something that can be easily tied and retied. For ties, use something besides traditional ribbons, try a jump rope, a lasso, or a favorite scarf. Cutouts can also be glued onto the boxes if more design or color is needed.

Toy Storage Baskets

Purchased at a dollar store, these baskets are not just for storing toys, but also double as building blocks for towers and containers for toss games. When the toys are put away, the baskets are stacked in a pyramid for space-saving and convenience.

Art Supply Jars

Jars purchased in a variety of sizes make terrific art supply keepers. Pencils, markers, crayons, paper clips, or erasers can be easily distinguished because the jars are transparent. Brightly colored jump ropes are wrapped and tied around the jars for safekeeping.

River's Bed

River loves to draw and ski, so coatrack hooks were attached onto my old skis for hanging toys, a hat, and River's New Year's resolution—a daily reminder of his goal. Each year, his favorite piece of art is framed with his school picture and his description of what he has drawn, then hung somewhere in the room. He loves to see how much better he is, year after year.

Jump Rope Clotheslines

Jump ropes as a design element are a constant theme in River's bedroom because he has always loved to jump rope—and is certain that he always will! Two jump ropes were strung in front of the upper portion of his window, and colorful clothespins hold his swim trunks on the line to dry while he sleeps. They are standard everyday wear for hot summer days.

Framed Letters

The letters spelling River's name are individually framed and hung above the window. The letters from an alphabet card game were enlarged and color-copied to the right size. Picture frames often go on closeout sales and can be painted to match any room. Inexpensive art from cards, books, or your children's drawings is easy to find.

Frame Tray

Old or new, frames make terrific useful trays for bedrooms or bathrooms. I used a wrapping paper with a brightly colored bug design to place behind the glass. Again, a child's artwork, wallpaper, fabric, or illustrations from books could be used. The pencil holder was made by River from baking clay, then painted with acrylic paints.

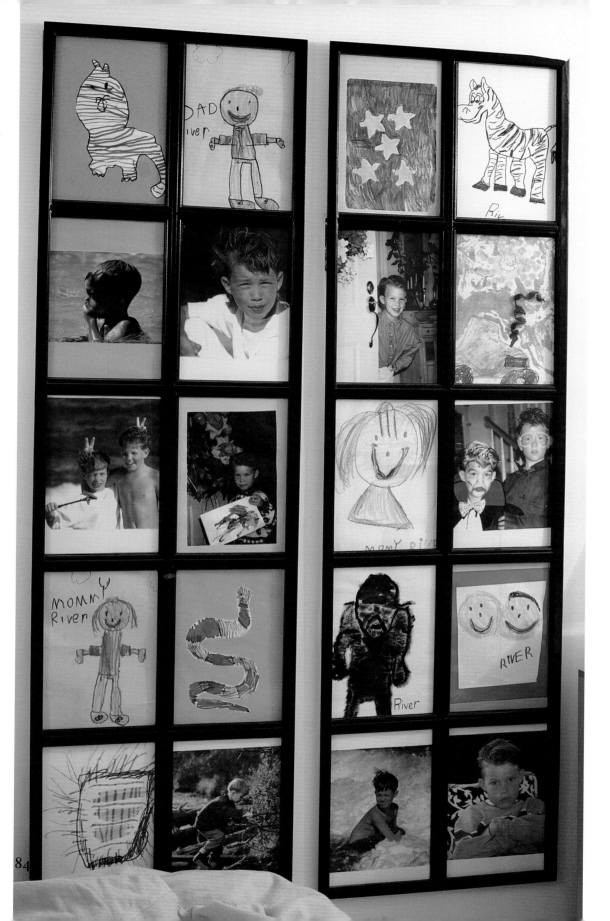

84

Art Wall

River also loves to draw and have his artwork displayed where he can see it everyday. Because he is such a prolific artist, I needed a large place to show his work. I came up with the idea of using these window grids, which I painted black, for presenting River's art and photos. The art is laminated and placed behind the grids with tiny nails, so it can be easily removed and replaced when a new favorite drawing or photo is created.

Four Mirrors

These colorful mirrors, with a
splash of yellow and blue back-
grounds, reminded me of our days
at the beach with the blue of the
ocean and the yellow of the sun-
shine on the sand. I purchased
them one rainy day when I was
shopping and came across a store
that was going out of business.

When redecorating River's room,
I wanted something to reach from
floor to ceiling in one corner, so I
stacked these mirrors four high.
With their vertical placement,
they act not only as a piece of art,
but as a full-length mirror.

With three active children and a husband who is a farmer, I spend a great deal of my time in my laundry room, so it is important to me that it be someplace I like to go. Someplace that is bright and cheery and makes me happy; and, as strange as it may seem, someplace that is filled with the things that I love.

My favorite part of the laundry room is the enormous yellow dandelion made for me by my youngest son to brighten my days of drudgery. It was made out of construction paper, so I had it laminated to hang on my door.

His yellow dandelion art inspired the three flowers I placed above the door. Each is actually an inexpensive plastic bowl with a juice strainer attached to the center.

laundry

Storage Buckets

Bright orange utility buckets make perfect storage containers for beach toys and cleaning supplies in my laundry room. Simply grab a bucket for a visit to the beach or for the chores around the house.

Polka Dots and Orange Clocks

I am not a lover of plain white walls, so I used a single large stencil to randomly stencil black polka dots on my laundry room walls.

Whenever I see a bargain and it is something I love, I purchase at least two—sometimes more. These two contemporary clocks give one last reminder of the time as we all go running out the door.

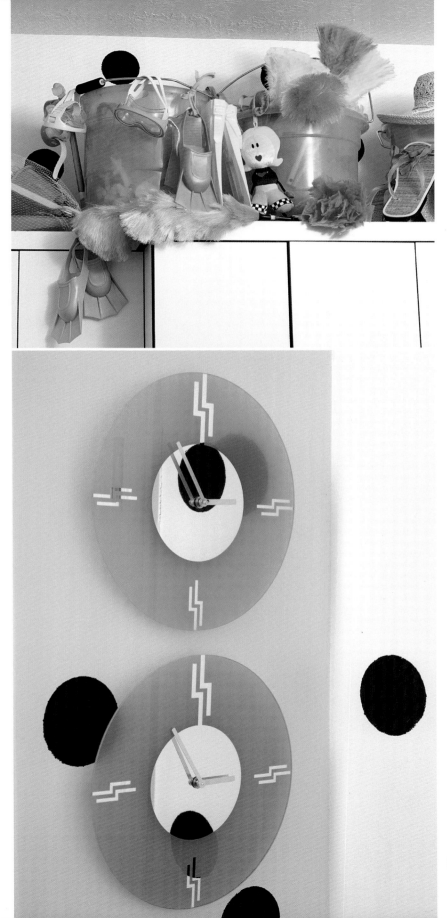

leopard
spots & pots

Each room in my house is a mixture of inspiration and evocation, imagination and expertise. And each mixture is highly adaptable to any room, anywhere. The lesson that is important for you to learn from what I do is that there really are no longer any rules to follow in design and decoration. You need only follow your instincts, choose what you like, spend as little as possible, collect as much as you can, use what you have in more than one way, and change it often.

I moved my dining room chairs into my living room, hung junk-store earrings from a scarf that is now a table runner, then gathered my favorite collection of beach paraphernalia together and put them in a corner of my family room. Here is a perfect example of how nothing need "match," of how to display what you like most, and of how to use something in more than one way. It is true dime-store decorating!

accessories

Scarf Table Runner

A scarf that I wear often is now being used as a table runner. When I wear it, the ends are unadorned; but while on the table, it has beaded earings pulled through the hem. This new accent takes only minutes to add.

Family Photographs

Treasured family photographs have even greater sentimental value when displayed in homemade frames. This particular frame has special meaning to me because it was made with seashells, gathered by my son Levi at the beach. He spent all day searching for the perfect shapes and colors. We returned home that day and glued them around an ordinary frame.

Bandanna Pillows

Ordinary items in dollar and discount stores can be put to extraordinary uses to add special accents to any decor. Two bandannas with leopard spots were folded in half and tied around two brightly colored pillows. A zebra-print scarf was tied in a bow around another pillow to coordinate with the animal-print theme. If you wanted to "dress things up," you could add pieces of jewelry.

Leopard Stairs

Everyone in our house loves leopard-print any-thing, so a leopard-print hall rug was tacked to the stairs leading from the dining room to our bedrooms. At the side of three of the stairs, ceramic mugs with colorful silk flowers were placed to make a statement in a small unex-pected place. The coffee mugs were converted to flowerpots by gluing a piece of florist foam in the cup and adding moss around the top.

Leopard-print Tabletop

Old discarded tables, which nobody wants but you, can be found at most rummage sales and flea markets. This was an old pine table. I decoupaged leopard-print tissue paper onto the tabletop and painted the legs black to accent the colors in the tissue. Decoupage is easy and inexpensive to do. Go to your local craft store, buy your favorite tissue, a bottle of decoupage glue, and follow the directions.

Decorated Lamp Shade

Dress up a lamp shade with inexpensive patterned scarves. These three printed scarves are a delicate accent when draped over the black-and-white striped lamp shade.

There are other fashion items that can be used to decorate lamp shades. Try strings of necklaces, lace hankies, woven belts, or tiny evening bags. Each adds an entirely new look.

Dime-store decorating on the table is like setting a stage. The table is a miniature theater of social behavior where a major portion of our lives is played out. It is here that stories are told, that problems are solved, that love blossoms, that careers are made, and that fortunes are

founded. The table is a place for sharing, for enjoyment, for celebration, and for discovery.

Anyone can set a table like a stage. The success of a table setting depends not on financial considerations, but on personal style and imagination. It is the soft luminous lighting from the candles that sets the mood at this dining-room table. Candleholders were made from margarita glasses with ponytail holders wrapped around the bases, or by turning wine glasses upside down, placing beaded jewelry inside and votive candles on top.

f o r m a l   d i n i n g

Salt Carriers

A delicate crystal perfume bottle is used on our table as a salt holder. Tiny vintage spoons found at my favorite antique store are used for dispensing the salt. The pepper mill with its more conventional lines is the perfect contrast for something so delicate and feminine.

Margarita Candleholders

When a margarita glass is filled with a tiny bit of water, a floating candle, and miniature blossoms, it is a heart-warming addition to any dining-room table. You can add as many as you like— they are so beautiful.

Perfect Place Settings

The foundation for this place setting in my animal-print dining room is a charger that is actually a mirror. It reflects not only the beauty of the table, but the soft golden glow of the candlelight. I used miniature picture frames for place cards. A picture of each guest or just their name may be written and placed inside the frame. The napkin rings are post earrings and lapel pins that have been fastened to each folded napkin. For additional ambience, a votive candle was placed inside a small clear glass filled with rock salt, then set on a miniature mirror to enhance the mirror chargers.

Whether you consider yourself a collector or not, the one cherishable of which you probably have many, is family photographs. Most of us want to keep our photos out where each occasion that is past can be relived time and time again. And most of us do not want to always frame each photograph in a traditional wooden frame. These unusual "frames" were made by using the glass pieces in the hutch in my dining room. "Frames" in the hutch on the left were made by having cherished old photos enlarged and photocopied to the right size, then placed inside cylindrical flower vases. Large square vases were also used as picture frames. However, this time, due to the size of the container, rice was poured inside to hold the photo in place. On the opposite page, lower right-hand corner, you will also see that small glasses were turned upside down, pictures were placed inside, and small tumblers were placed on top. Matching soap dispensers have had tiny flowers added to them for an overall hutch accent.

Cake Plates

Serving food is as much a part of decorating as the various accessories that are always on display. Delicious chocolate cake and muffins are a part of a fabulous presentation when placed on this black-and-white chessboard—now serving tray. A large slice of cake is served on a small black-and-white plate that was set on top of a candleholder's metal base. Soap dishes were used for the muffin plates, and a bathroom soap dispenser became the base for a second muffin plate by removing the pump and hot-gluing the soap dish on the top. The matching bathroom tumbler is used for serving hot cocoa.

Black-and-White Cake Plate

This cake plate was made by decoupaging black-and-white polka-dotted paper to the back of a clear glass plate. The decoupaged plate was then sprayed with a sealant. The cake plate was hot-glued to the an inverted bathroom tumbler.

FAIRY TALES DO COME TRUE

Wish upon a star!

Day-to-day chores of every housewife, mother, or grown-up almost always include duties that need a desk. Paying bills, writing thank-you notes, sending party invitations—each needs special consideration and undivided attention. Adjacent to my kitchen, I had a desk built for just such tasks. Like all other areas in my home, this one, too, needed to have my dime-store-decorating touches. The window-like mirror added space and light to a small area, and the addition of coffee-mug coasters created a silhouetted look when I attached them to and above the mirror. I, of course, have my favorite sayings both above me and beneath me, and my chair is backed with seashells strung on a ribbon.

desk

Desk Accessories

My favorite mugs are used for pencil holders and bookends, while a napkin holder, turned upside down, contains my desk clutter easily and efficiently. I found this whimsical little clock in a very nice gift store; but it had been damaged, so the owner was selling it below her cost. Anything can be fixed, so I immediately bought it and took it home for the needed repairs.

Bulletin Board

I could not find a bulletin board small enough that I liked, so I made my own. It is a wooden picture frame with the glass removed, and a piece of cork stapled to the back. The pins are also ones I made by gluing thumbtacks to the back of some of my favorite trinkets. I have a wooden heart that I especially like, that always holds my most important notes.

Whether indoors or outdoors, flowerpots have so many uses that they are truly one of the best dime-store buys. Whenever you see pots you

like, at a price you can afford, buy them and keep them for another day. They can be painted, stained, or decoupaged to make beautiful gifts filled with potted plants. Pots can become the package for a gift by being filled with tissue and wrapped tightly with ribbons; they can be the dishes for baking fresh bread or muffins; or they can become bowls to serve salads and soups, hors d'oeuvres, or treats.

These plain terra-cotta flowerpots are a perfect example. They are gifts for friends to take home from a recipe party, and they are to be used to serve their contents at the receiver's dinner table. Even the trays are used for little serving dishes.

flowerpots

Plant Stand

This flea-market discovery makes a unique and quite functional plant stand for the cheerful potted plants and flowers in my yard.

Simple terra-cotta flowerpots and rustic tin pails complement the colors of the old stove as well as the plants that grow around it.

Moss Flowerpots

Flowerpots need not always be made of clay or porcelain or metal. They can be as these are—plastic watering cans and pots, covered with moss. The moss is simply glued to the outside of the container with a cold-glue gun. In the summer the flowers may be real and in the winter they may not.

go ahead
with red

A celebration of the simplicity, warmth, and enduring charm of the American rural tradition is what my kitchen is to me. It is the pieces of the stories from America's heartland, it is the colors of the seasons from shore to shore, it is the undisputed essence of my favorite collections.

Collectors and antique purists may surround themselves with nothing but authentic furnishings and accessories from one particular period or style. However, the style of a more broadly based collector such as myself is one that springs from a common rural tradition, one that is versatile, and one that is eclectic by nature. When an eclectic collection has a common thread, it gives a room a unique decorative stamp, and the common thread of this collection is the color red. Even though I adore all of these pieces, my favorite is the red shoes that occupy the top shelf. They alone tell a treasured story and remind us all that, "there is no place like home."

cupboards

Red Finial Accents

This cheery yellow picnic basket, two red finials, and an old gift tin were a great choice for that extra splash of color needed above my kitchen cupboards. Red and gray paint was applied to the unfinished finials to achieve an aged look. To add extra height, I stacked one finial on a tin.

Lacy Shelf Liners

The look of lace hanging over the shelf in the cupboard is so charming and delicate, it reminds me of my great grandmother. Lace fabric scraps, vintage lace purchased at the thrift store, or bargain-store closeouts provide inexpensive shelf liners that can be changed often and easily.

Picture Frames

Any inexpensive, ordinary picture frame can be easily decorated. Simply paint the frame in the color of your choice. In the top frame to the left, the mat was removed and an additional piece of glass was added so that the greeting card was sandwiched between two pieces of glass. On the bottom frame, polka dots were added by dipping a pencil eraser into white paint and pressing onto the frame. Designs other than polka dots can be quickly and easily added by the use of stencils, stickers, or stamps. This is a wonderfully inexpensive way to hang your own and your family's favorite greeting cards and photographs.

My family is the essence of American spirit: independent individuals with spontaneity, ingenuity, and a healthy sense of humor. That style which is ours celebrates America's greatest resource—the family. Our family style is all about the from-the-heart details that make a house a home, and guests feel like family. We pride ourselves in our unique family treasures that we give and collect, our stylish and effortless entertaining, and our treasure trove of ideas for every season of the year.

During the summer months we often have friends, neighbors, and family over for good-old-American barbecues. Because we love dessert the most—and sometimes eat it first—it is always set for whoever, whenever they want it. And because we live in the country, the spirit is casual and unexpected. On this particular summer day, the wind was blowing, so I took large hair clips and used them to secure the tablecloth to the picnic table. Brightly painted napkin rings in fish shapes were slid over the upper teeth of the hairclips to add a touch of the ocean we love.

outdoors

This bedroom is fun and colorful and perfect for my son Levi, who loves sports of all kinds. Above his bed hangs a volleyball net filled with his favorite toys—balls. Nearly every kind of ball in every color and size, can be found in this oversized, basketball-type net. The net is secured to the ceiling with 2" hook screws to prevent any middle-of-the-night releases!

The headboard is actually large wooden pencils attached directly to the wall. I purchased several of these at a discount store in the back-to-school section. I used baseballs with the red pencil headboard to remind Levi you must go to school and do well in order to be part of the team.

I purchased old golf clubs at a garage sale and putters at a used sports equipment store to make his name on the wall. The putters were cut with a pipe cutter to make the "E."

sports room

118

Pictures for the Wall

Levi loves outdoor winter sports and he has just taken up snowshoe-ing. He was with me one Saturday morning at a garage sale and found these in a pile. They were his first garage sale purchase and immediately went on his wall, when we returned home.

Bed End Table

Levi's old red wagon placed on a trunk makes a wonderful end table for keeping books, toys, and a red lava lamp. The trunk is one that was his grandfather's and is now used for storage. The wagon brings back happy memories for him as a very young child.

Baseball Pillows

Black plaid pillows with baseballs as buttons continue the sports theme in the details that are so important. I used a needle with very strong thread and repeatedly stitched through the stitching on the baseball, then through the pillow, and then through a large button on the other side of the pillow, until the baseball was fastened securely.

School Books

At Levi's school, all of the students' books must be wrapped in paper to protect the covers, so Levi wrapped his in wrapping paper that he picked out at the closeout store.

With a pride in country and family, we redecorated Laci's first bedroom to be a guest room with a spirit and a proud heritage. We sometimes have guests who come from other countries and we want them to experience an American style of decorating, so we added touches of red, white, and blue.

The vintage iron bed frame was purchased at a rummage sale and even though it needed some repair and a coat of paint, it was a bargain and exactly what Laci wanted. The umbrella headboard was purchased at an end-of-season sale for a minimal price, and adds an unexpected touch.

The red-and-white plaid pillows were made by folding a dishtowel in half and sewing three seams and attaching three red ribbon bows. The "L" shaped pillow, however, is very special because it was made from the fabric of a dress long since outgrown.

red & white room

Trellis Photo Frame

A white garden trellis is attached to the wall with small nails in several places. Laci now attaches the photographs of herself and guests who visit our home with red thumbtacks purchased in any school supply section. If you want to avoid putting holes in your photos they may be attached with photo putty that can be purchased at office supply stores.

Curtain Valance

A red plaid dish towel was placed above the window and tied to the curtain rod with additional smaller gingham dish towels.

Red Purse

The adorable red purse tied with a big bow was one of those impulsive purchases in one of Laci's favorite stores.

Kitties Blackboard

Kitty corkboards that were purchased in a case-lot sale were used to create a border for this blackboard. I measured the distance of a specific number of kitties, then marked off a section of the wall and painted it with blackboard paint. The kitties were then mounted onto the wall with small nails to create the border. This is where we leave messages for our out-of-town guest. However, when the guestroom is not in use, Laci's friends will often leave messages for her.

The Three Bears

These sweet valentine chairs were found at a discount store at a wonderful after-holiday sale. They were marked down considerably because some of the paint had been chipped off. I bought some red acrylic paint and Laci repainted the chairs and added tiny white polka dots with a small pencil eraser.

Since Laci loves the story of the three bears, she purchased three that would fit nicely on each chair. She did, however, leave a special chair for Goldilocks, but the deal is she must not come over too often.

think
pink

The essence of an eclectic style of decorating is the combination old fabrics and textures with modern comforts and character. The essence of a teenage daughter is the combination of all-grown-up and still daddy's-little-girl with whatever is popular today, not yesterday or tomorrow!

Laci helped me decorate her new bedroom—it had to be her, it had to be loved by her friends, and it had to be easy to change (because what is important today is old news tomorrow). A wedding dress purchased at a thrift store was taken apart for better use. The skirt was attached to the wall above the headboard, and the bodice was made into matching pillows. One pillow used the dress's tie as decoration, and the second pillow used the buttons down the back to adorn the pillow front. A pink feather boa was attached to the edges of a third pillow for a little fun and fluff!

pink room

Bedroom Furniture and Accessories

This photo is all about pink gingham tablecloths—my daughter's favorite. I cut one up, and made two very cute covers for the plain white stools in Laci's room, and then with what was left over, I trimmed the bottom of her jeans. For the stool covers, I cut the cloth in squares and simply tied large pink bows around each leg.

The suitcases were throw-a-ways that were salvaged, painted white, and are now used for storage—something a teenager never has enough of. And sometimes, everything does not always get put inside—her dancing shoes rest on top. She believes that is where they need to be.

The cement floor was painted with porch paint—first white, then I taped off the squares with painter's tape and painted them pink.

Magnet Board

This was a mirror that had been broken and discarded so I retrieved it and put a piece of sheet metal in the frame where the mirror had been. Laci uses this board to hold her favorite pictures, one of which is a little girl in pink, who is now her Grandma Grover. As a way to hold the photos and messages in place, Laci attached round magnets to the back of her Grandmother Grover's vintage earrings. This picture with its special earring magnets will probably be the only thing that never changes on Laci's board.

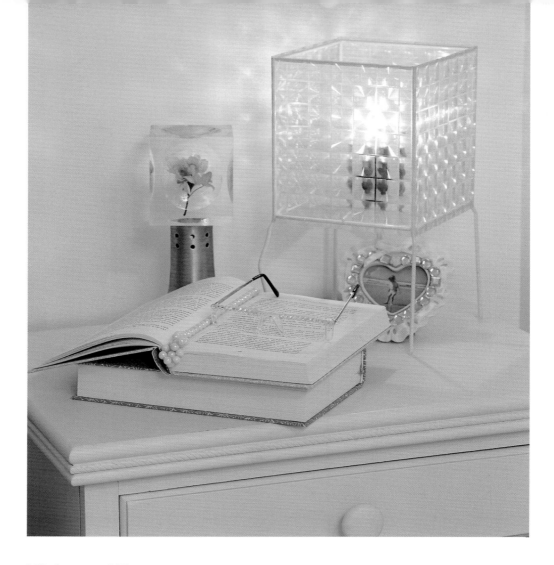

Nightstand Treasures

This small heart frame was broken when purchased, so after it was repaired, it was embellished with pink rhinestones, to not only hide the flaw, but add sparkle to a very pretty room. Reading glasses with tiny rhinestones glued on the rim are placed on the open book, and can be used as a bookmark if the old pink necklace bookmark is lost. Rhinestones were also added to the frames in the photo on the left, and a ballet tutu was placed over the all-white lamp shade. As I have seen done in expensive decorating stores, I added small pink silk flowers between the netting for detail.

Crystal Knobs for Drawers and Cabinets

These drawer pulls were made from crystal votive candleholders. A small wooden knob was painted white and sprinkled with iridescent confetti glitter before being glued to the inside of the candleholder. The candleholder was then secured to the cabinet or drawer with industrial-strength glue.

Slipper Picture

These very funky bright pink slippers with yellow and blue flowers were glued to a baking sheet and sit "quietly" in Laci's window. I am not certain why she loves these—but she does. The muffin tin is filled with her hair clips, bath beads, soap and scrubbing puff. She picks this up and takes it with her to the bathroom each morning to get ready for the school day.

Bathroom Scale

Rhinestones can put a little glitter and gleam on ordinary everyday objects that need a bit of touching up. Here, a bathroom scale has been adorned with blue and pink rhinestones and a spring bracelet around the edges for a fun and somewhat crazy look. A soap dispenser is also adorned with rhinestones, resembling glistening bubbles around the top.

The soft and flattering color of pink is the perfect color for women to decorate with . . . it brings into play the gentle warmth of the new season's sun and the spirit of spring. This very feminine and welcoming breakfast table was an ideal place for Sunday brunch and a parade of pink.

A wire basket and a small purse hold pink paper plates. An angel food cake, with a hint of pink food coloring and marshmallow drizzle atop, was placed on the tabletop and accompanied by a napkin, rolled and tied with a soft pink sequin trim. A pink rose from the garden was placed inside the stark white vase, and a pale pink pearl necklace was wrapped gently around its neck. A single rose was also placed inside an elegant crystal jar to float in water tinted with a tiny bit of pink food coloring and scented with rose petal perfume.

table setting

Party Favors

I always love to buy holiday treasures because they serve as wonderful party favors. Here, the small pink Easter eggs that fill this wire basket have been filled with Easter grass, candy kisses, barrettes, and a tiny photograph. Each brunch guest will be given one to take home.

Pink Party Ware

The flatware for the party has been placed in a toothbrush holder, and a bathroom tumbler holds a stack of paper cups neatly.

Flower Vase

The small flower vase is actually a beaded lamp shade, turned upside down and set in a silver tumbler. Earrings were fastened to the side of the lamp shade, and small pink flowers were set inside.

The beautiful ballet picture looks simply elegant in the white frame and pink mat. I purchased two ballet pictures preframed in small inexpensive metal frames. I removed the pictures from the frame and placed them in a very large frame with an oversized pink mat. The larger frame was an inexpensive wood frame that was painted white, and I had a professional cut the mat. Whenever you have a large wall area and cannot afford to cover it with expensive art, try this technique of framing small cards, prints, or photographs in very big mats and frames. Some of the frames can even be left empty. Paint all of the frames the same color, remove the glass and mat and hang from a nail in a grouping of empty frames.

details

Unusual Vases

Pink hydrangeas look beautiful here in flour sifter vases. A small cup of water was placed inside each sifter to keep the flowers fresh and hold them in place. Two small white mugs sitting on top of each other make another unusual but beautiful vase for the white roses. The bottom mug was turned upside down and the top mug was hot-glued to secure it in place.

Silver Candleholders

Not all "silver" candleholders need be expensive and purchased in fine gift stores. These are made from precut pieces of heat-vent pipes that are found in any hardware or home improvement store. They come in predetermined lengths with crimped ends, so your candlesticks may all be one length or a variety of lengths. Take the pipe with you when you purchase candles for a proper fit.

Rain Gauge Candleholders

These rain gauges were purchased at a local dollar store, and the plastic containers were replaced with crystal candleholders for delicate outdoor lighting. Inside the glass candleholders, water and small floating candles were placed. When arranged near the hydrangeas, these floating votive candles make a shimmering statement.

index